50 Cent – A CANDID BIOGRAPHY OF A SELF-MADE HUSTLER:

THE LIFE AND TIMES OF CURTIS "50 Cent" JACKSON; RAPPER, SINGER, SONGWRITER, ACTOR, ENTREPRENEUR, INVESTOR.

By JJ Vance

Table of Contents

Before You Go Any Further,
Download Your Free Gift!

Thanks for checking out **"50 Cent – A CANDID BIOGRAPHY OF A SELF-MADE HUSTLER"** – You have made a wise choice in picking up this book!

Because you're about to discover many interesting tidbits of 50 Cent you've never knew before!

But before you go any further, I'd like to offer you a free gift.

My Ultimate Collection of Links to 50 Cent's YouTube Videos!

If you're a 50 Cent fan, you'll DROOL over this!

But I'll take it down if too many people claim it as it's my personal treasure. *Don't miss out!*

Get it before it expires here:
https://bit.ly/50CentBonus
Or Scan the QR Code:

50 Cent Introduction and Background

Curtis James Jackson III, most popularly known by his stage name "50 Cent", is one of the few people in the entertainment industry who have attained the "legend" status while still young and alive. Curtis' legend status is very well deserved. The entertainer is pretty versatile in his talents and has put them all to very good use, collecting tons of awards and accolades along the way.

His talents in the art span across singing, rapping, songwriting, acting, and producing. Apart from his artistic talents, Curtis Jackson is also very well known for his very successful entrepreneurial exploits.

In this book, we are going to take an in-depth look at Curtis "50 Cent" Jackson in all areas of his professional life.

His Early Life

Curtis James Jackson III was born on July 6, 1975, in Queens, New York City to his father and mother, Sabrina. He was raised by his drug dealer mother in the South Jamaica area of Queens until she passed away when he was eight years old. According to reports, his mother passed away in a mysterious fire accident. After Sabrina's death, Curtis' father left and the responsibility of raising him fell on to his grandmother, who did just that.

Curtis began to pick up an interest in boxing when he was around eleven years old. By the time he was 14, he was spending most of his free time in the boxing gym that a neighbor built for the local youth. When he was not in the gym sparring, he admits to either being in school or peddling crack on the strip. He believes that his competitiveness in the boxing sport helped him in his rap career as the rap industry is pretty competitive.

Jackson's grandparents found out about his drug-dealing escapades after he was arrested for bringing guns and drugs to school in the tenth grade. He was arrested many more times after that for various drugs and gun-related offenses, including selling cocaine to a police officer who was working undercover at the time. He was eventually sentenced to prison for up to nine years but only served six months in a boot camp. Jackson was eventually able to get his GED despite all the trouble he got into.

50 Cent THE RAPPER

His Early Career

Although 50 Cent only rose to fame in 2003 through his debut album *'Get Rich or Die Tryin'*, he actually started his rap career as early as 1996. He began by rapping in his friend's basement and using basic and amateur instruments to record over instrumentals. He did not make much progress until 1996 when he was introduced to Jam Master Jay by a friend. Jam Master Jay (real name: Jason William Mizell) was a musician and DJ and was part of a music group called Run-D. M. C. — one of the biggest hip hop groups of that time, so this was a very big deal for 50 Cent.

Jam Master Jay gave Jackson an audience and listened to some of his rap. He was very impressed by him, especially because he did most of the work on his own. In fact, Jam Master Jay was impressed by Jackson enough to take him under his wings and show him the ins and outs of the industry. Jackson credited Jam Master Jay for teaching him how to produce his records, write choruses, and write bars and hooks, amongst other things. 50 Cent eventually joined his record label, Jam Master Jay Records. While under the label, Jackson got his first feature opportunity on Onyx's 1998 album, *'Shut 'Em Down'*. He was on a track titled *'React'*. Jam Master eventually produced an album for 50 Cent, but it unfortunately never saw the light of day.

50 Cent's Brief Stint with the Trackmasters/Columbia Records

Since nothing came out of 50 Cent's deal with Jam Master Jay, he moved on and aligned himself with 'Trackmasters' —a team of two music producers Poke (real name: Jean-Claude Olivier) and Tone (real name: Samuel Barnes). They were pretty hot in the late

1900s and early 2000s; so hot in fact that their record label,

Columbia Records, let them have their own imprint label,

Trackmasters Entertainment. In the year 2000, Trackmasters signed

50 Cent to this imprint label at Columbia records. The label sent him

to a better, upscale studio for two weeks, where he proceeded to

produce what was supposed to be his debut album, *'Power of the

Dollar'*. He recorded 36 songs while at the studio but included only

18 in the album. The album consisted of tracks like *'Ghetto Qur'an

(Forgive Me)'*, *'How to Rob'*, and *'Thug Love'* which featured girl

group, Destiny's Child.

      'How to Rob' was pre-released as a single in August 1999 and

in it, 50 Cent details how he would rob famous artists/celebrities.

The celebrities he mentioned in the song include Kirk Franklin, Boyz II

Men, Michael Bivins, Heavy D, Mister Cee, DMX, Timbaland, Missy

Elliott, Blackstreet, Juvenile, TQ, Joe, Sticky Fingaz, Canibus, Busta

Rhymes, the Flipmode Squad, Mike Tyson, Robin Givens, Fredro

Starr, RZA, Ghostface Killah, DJ Clue, Raekwon, Will Smith, Jada

Pinkett Smith, Jermaine Dupri, Da Brat, Treach, P Diddy, Whitney Houston, Bobby Brown, Jay Z, Trackmasters, Stevie J, Slick Rick, Big Pun, Kurupt, Foxy Brown, Mase, Harlem World, Cardan, Lil' Kim, Brian McKnight, Keith Sweat, Ol' Dirty Bastard, Master P, Silkk The Shocker and R Kelly. The original version of the song also mentions R&B singer Case Woodward and his ex Mary J. Blige and Mariah Carey and her ex-husband, Tommy Mottola. Mariah Carey did not like that her name was in the song and threatened to leave the record label if it wasn't removed.

The single created a lot of publicity for 50 Cent and his upcoming album, *'Power of the Dollar'*. He emphasized that the song was not to be taken seriously and several of the artists mentioned on the song responded in songs of their own at later times. Jay Z, Sticky Fingaz, Big Pun, Kurupt, Missy Elliott all responded in different ways to the track. The track entered the U.S. Billboard Hot R&B/Hip Hop Songs chart and peaked at number 62. It also entered the U.S. Billboard Hot Rap Singles chart and peaked at number 24. It was generally well received. His popularity began to grow off the success of the track, and he got an invite to join Nas on his Nostradamus tour.

Again, 50 Cent's second album never saw the light of day as trouble struck three days before the music video for *'Thug Love'* was scheduled to be shot. 50 Cent was near his grandmother's home in South Jamaica, New York City, on May 24, 2000, when he was attacked, robbed and shot. The severe shooting incident saw 50 Cent with nine life-threatening bullet wounds. He was shot in the hand, face, right and left legs, arm, hip, chest and cheek. He spent about two weeks in the hospital and ended up losing a tooth, having a swollen tongue and slurred voice, but he survived. Mike Tyson's close friend and bodyguard, Darryl Baum, was the alleged attacker, and he was killed three days after the attack. The shooting incident became quite a defining moment in 50 Cent's career, and it's mentioned in quite a number of his future tracks.

The shooting incident was assumed to be a result of 50 Cent's past involvement with drugs, guns and gangs. This brought quite bad publicity and it eventually jeopardized the deal he had with Trackmasters/Columbia Records. They did not like the negative press surrounding him and dropped out of their deal with him, thereby putting a halt to the release of the *'Power of the Dollar'* album they had been working on. This turn of events severely strained Jackson's relationship with Trackmasters, Poke (Jean-Claude Olivier) and Tone (Samuel Barnes). Additionally, Trackmasters were producing Jennifer Lopez's *'I'm Gonna be Alright'* remix and it was scheduled for release and included a feature from 50 Cent. The shooting incident, along with the fact that 50 Cent was not very popular at the time, led to him being quickly replaced by Nas, who he was friends with, on the project. This led to a small beef with Nas and further escalated his problems with Trackmasters. Their relationship soured and they stopped working together.

Being Blacklisted and Getting Back On Track

50 Cent got out of the hospital with no record deal and had been blacklisted by the recording industry because of his track, *'Ghetto Qur'an'*. In the song, he mentions the names of drug dealers from the South Jamaica area of Queens where he grew up and it was not taken well. Kenneth 'Supreme' McGriff, a convicted drug lord and friend of the music industry at the time did not like what 50 Cent had done and blacklisted him. The IRS also believed that the shooting incident was 'punishment' for the song that detailed the Kenneth McGriff's drug dealing business.

50 Cent took the fact that he had survived this severe shooting as a sign that his life had a greater purpose and began to pursue a new lease on life. He went back to the rap underground and formed a rap group, G-Unit, which included Lloyd Banks and Tony Yayo. Since he had been blacklisted from recording music in the US, he went to Canada with Sha Money XL, his business partner. He

worked hard, churning out mix tape upon mix tape with the backing of his group, G-Unit. His popularity steadily came back and he released the *'Guess Who's Back?'* mix tape on April 26, 2002.

The mix tape featured songs that had been originally scheduled to be released on his *'Power of the Dollar'* album with Columbia records. It included songs like *'Your Life's on the Line'*, *'Corner Bodega'*, *'As the World Turns'* and *Ghetto Qur'an* rereleased as *'Ghetto Qua ran'*. It was his first official release after several foiled attempts with first, Jay Master Jay records and then Columbia Records. Several producers worked on by several producers, including Trackmasters, Kurt Gowdy, Fantom of the Beat, Terrence Dudley, Red Spyda, Sha Money XL (who doubled as his business partner), DJ Clark Kent and Father Shaheed.

The mix tape was positively received by the general public and critics alike, peaked at number 28 on the U.S. Billboard 200 chart, and sold over four hundred thousand copies in the United

States. Eminem discovered 50 Cent through this mix tape and sought to help him get signed to a record label. Eminem flew him to Los Angeles to meet Dr. Dre, and they eventually signed to both of their record labels, Shady records and Aftermath Entertainment for a deal worth one million dollars. 50 Cent recorded one more mix tape with his group, G-Unit before moving on. They released *'No Mercy, No Fear'* on August 1, 2002 and the mix tape contained hit single, *'Wanksta'*. The mix tape featured on XXL's Top 20 Mix tapes list and was peaked at No. 5. Once the G-Unit mix tape was done, 50 Cent moved on to record and release his debut album, *'Get Rich or Die Tryin'*.

His Official Debut Album; 'Get Rich or Die Tryin'.

The *'Get Rich or Die Tryin'* album is one of the most iconic rap albums of all time, and it broke several records when it was released in February 2003. It was released as a joint effort between Shady Records, G-Unit Records, Aftermath Entertainment and Interscope Records. It was mostly executively produced by 50 Cent, Eminem and Dr. Dre with creative support from other producers like Sha Money XL (who was also an executive producer), and a host of many others. The album featured some members of his G-unit crew, Tony Yayo & Lloyd Banks. The album also got Eminem, Snoop Dogg, and Nate Dogg featuring on the album.

The album contained 16 tracks and 3 bonus tracks with the most successful single being the track 'In Da Club', The album had several pre-released songs as bonus tracks including 'Wanksta' that was previously released on the 'No Mercy, No Fear' mix tape, 'U Not Like Me' and 'Life's on the Line'. The album was released in different countries with different bonus tracks, with 'In Da Club' (Instrumental) and 'Soldier' (Freestyle) (featuring G-Unit) in Japan and 'In Da Club' (acapella) in the United Kingdom.

50 Cent's *'Get Rich or Die Tryin'* album was very favorably received by music critics within the rap industry. The album garnered amazing reviews from platforms like Metacritic (rated 73 out of 100), AllMusic (rated 4 stars out of 5), Blender (rated 4 stars out of 5), Entertainment Weekly (rated it a B), The Guardian (3 stars out of 5), Los Angeles Times(3 stars out of 4), Pitchfork (scored it 7/10), Q (4 stars out of 5), Rolling Stone (4 stars out of 5), USA Today (3 stars out of 4), XXL (a score of 5 out of 5), etc. 50 Cent himself as well as his album were praised by critics for his persona, rap style, storytelling and versatility.

The album ranked reasonably well on music charts with Billboard Magazine pegging it at No. 12 on the Top 200 Albums of the decade. *'In the Da Club'*, one of singles off the album peaked at number one on Billboard Magazine's 2003 single and album of the year. *'Back Down'*, another single off the album was acknowledged as one of the greatest diss tracks of all time by XXL. The entire album also made the Billboard Magazine Top 200 Albums of All Time, ranked at number 139.

The album was a huge commercial success, making its debut at No. 1 on the Billboard 200 list and selling nearly 900,000 copies within the first week of release. It eventually sold over 12 million copies worldwide by the end of 2003. The Recording Industry Association of America in 2003 certified the album 6x platinum for selling over 6 million copies in the United States. It eventually went 9x Platinum in the United States The album went Gold in several countries out of the U.S. (France, Germany, Greece, Japan, New Zealand, Norway and Sweden), Platinum in Belgium, Ireland and Switzerland, 2x Platinum in Australia, 3x Platinum in Denmark, and Russia, 4x Platinum in the United Kingdom and 6x Platinum in Canada. Several of the tracks on the album reached number one on the U.S. music charts with P.I.M.P. topping charts internationally.

The album was nominated for several awards including Best Rap Album at the 46th Grammy Awards (which it didn't win), Favorite Rap/Hip Hop Album at the 2003 American Music Awards (AMAs) (which it won), and Top Billboard 200 Album at the 2003 Billboard Music Awards (which it also won).

G-Unit Records

Following the huge success of 50 Cent's debut album, *'Get Rich or Die Tryin'* in 2003; Interscope records gave him his own record label which he named G-Unit Records. His first signees were his group mates, Lloyd Banks and Tony Yayo. He also signed Young Buck who featured on his album. Each rapper was signed as both an individual artist and part of the group, G-Unit.

The group released their debut work, *'Beg for Mercy'* in November 2003, just nine months after the release of Jackson's album. Although group member Tony Yayo was in prison at the time the album was being recorded serving time for gun possession and jumping bail, he still contributed to the creative process. The album was produced by a host of notable producers like Dr Dre, Megahertz, 7th EMP, Big-Toni, Black Jeruz and host of many others. Even 50 Cent also had producing credit on the album has he also contributed in the production of the work.

The album contains 19 tracks including *'G-Unit'*, *'Poppin' Them Thangs'*, ' *'Wanna Get to Know You'* featuring Joe, *'Groupie Love'* featuring Butch Cassidy. Several songs on the album were samples of some popular songs at the time.

The album was very well received by critics and got great reviews from platforms like Metacritic, Allmusic, Entertainment Weekly, Robert Christgau, RapReviews.com, Blender, E!, Popmatters and Rollingstone. It made its debut at No. 3 on the Billboard 200 list and sold almost 400,000 copies in its first week of release. As of April

2008, the album had sold over 6 million copies worldwide and had gone 2x Platinum, certified The Recording Industry Association of America (RIAA). The album also went Platinum in the United Kingdom and 4x Platinum in both Canada and the United States.

After the album had been recorded, the record label signed The Game and Spider Loc in early 2004. 50 Cent's relationship with the game however was quite tumultuous and they eventually parted ways. The way 50 Cent's relationship with The Game turned out made him reevaluate his decision to sign people he did not consider as family into the record label. The record label still went on to sign several acts including Young Hot Rod, Nyce, 40 Glocc and Mazaradi Fox.

Talks of problems in the G-Unit group started in 2008. According to rumors, 50 Cent had kicked Young Buck out of the group. 50 Cent came out to confirm the rumors but assured the public that even though he had been kicked out of the group, Young

Buck was still signed to the record label. The result of this was a rivalry and back and forth between the two artists. Young Buck joined forces with former group member, The Game, and released diss songs against 50 Cent. It turned out that Young Buck owed 50 Cent some money and that was the beginning of their problems. The whole feud eventually settled down by the end of 2008.

50 Cent's Subsequent Works

50 Cent released other bodies of work in 2005, 2007 and 2009; *'The Massacre', 'Curtis'* and *'Before I Self Destruct'. 'The Massacre'* was released on the 3rd of March, 2005 and contained 22 tracks. It contained some of 50 Cent's most iconic and major hits to date. 50 Cent featured his usual array of artists on this album. Artists like Olivia, Lloyd Banks, Young Buck, The Game, Jamie Foxx, Tony Yayo and Eminem. The tracks on the album include; *'Intro', 'In My Hood', 'This is 50', 'I'm Supposed to Die Tonight', 'Build You Up'* featuring Jamie Foxx, *'God Gave Me Style', 'So Amazing'* featuring

Olivia, *'I Don't Need Em'* and *'Hate It or Love It'* featuring Lloyd

Banks, Young Buck, The Game and Tony Yayo.

The album was quite successful as it debuted at No. 1 on the

US Billboard 200 and sold about 1.2 million copies within its very first

week. The album was nominated for the Best Rap Album award at

the 48th Grammy awards but did not win. The album sold over 9

million copies worldwide and went Platinum in several countries

including Australia, Canada, Germany, Ireland, New Zealand, Russia,

Switzerland, the United Kingdom and the United States.

50 Cent's next album was *'Curtis'*, named after him. *'Curtis'*

was released on September 11, 2007 and contained 17 tracks. The

album featured several artists, including Mary J. Blige, Tony Yayo,

Young Buck, Nicole Scherzinger, Eminem and Dr. Dre. The tracks on

'Curtis' include; *'Intro'*, *'My Gun Go Off'*, *'Man Down'*, *'I'll Still Kill'*, *'I*

Get Money', *'Come and Go'* featuring Dr. Dre, *'Ayo Technology'*,

'Follow My Lead', *'Movin on Up'*, *'Straight to the Bank'*, *'Amusement*

Park', 'Fully Loaded Clip', 'Peep Show' featuring Eminem, 'Fire' featuring Young Buck and Nicole Scherzinger, 'All of Me' featuring Mary J. Blige, 'Curtis 187' and 'Touch the Sky' featuring Tony Yayo. The album had 50 Cent's usual tones of street confidence, thug, sexy and tough.

Although this album did not do as well as 50 Cent's previous works, it still had quite a reasonable amount of success, debuting at No. 2 on the US Billboard 200 chart and selling about 700,000 copies within the first week of release. It topped several charts in several countries and went Gold and Platinum in several countries as well.

Curtis '50 Cent' Jackson continued to release hit singles and albums. In total he has released five studio albums: ('Get Rich or Die Tryin' (2003), 'The Massacre' (2005), 'Curtis' (2005), 'Before I Self Destruct' (2007), 'Animal Ambition' (2014)), four compilation albums('24 Shots' (2003), 'Best Of' (2017) amongst others), two video albums ('Get Rich or Die Tryin' (2003) and '50 Cent: The New Breed' (2003), eighty-eight music videos, two movie soundtrack albums [*'Get Rich or Die Tryin'* (2005) and *'Southpaw'* (2015)] and ten mix tapes [*'Guess Who's Back'* (April 2002), *'50 Cent is the Future'* (June 2002), *'No Mercy, No Fear'* (August 2002), *'God's Plan'* (October 2002), *'Bullet Proof'* (2005), *'War Angel'* (June 2009), *'Forever King'* (July 2009), *'The Big 10'* (December 2011), *'The Lost Tape'* (May 2012), *'The Kanan Tape'* (December 2015)]

Curtis '50 Cent' Jackson achieved all of these while simultaneously managing his record label and other business ventures. He eventually diversified and ventured into film acting, producing, podcast shows amongst others.

50 Cent THE ACTOR

50 Cent has featured in seventeen different movies! As well as his classic *Get Rich Or Die Tryin,* he is also featured in: *Home of the Brave, Righteous Kill, Before I Self Destruct, Streets of Blood, Dead Man Running, Caught in the Crossfire, 13, Gun, Twelve, Blood Out, Setup, All Things Fall Apart, Crossfire, Fire with Fire, Escape Plan, Oath.*

In the wake of climbing to stardom, 50 took advantage of YouTube as an exhibit for his material that just couldn't stand by to adhere to customary procedures. This generally comprises of natively constructed recordings in which he wears senseless outfits, talks in senseless voices, and mugs his way through apparently comic vignettes. His YouTube character is Pimpin' Curly, a procurer of whores with Eriq LaSalle's hair from Coming To America and a voice out of a blaxploitation film.

Pimpin' Curly wasn't the only channel that 50 used to express his creativity. Jackson additionally took what gave off an impression of being his grandmother's camcorder and composed, coordinated, and featured in the madly terrible Before I Self Destruct, a DVD of which was incorporated with his music album which had the same title. His fans were sorely disappointed with the storyline which revolved around an athlete who gets involved in gang-related violence, while also trying to take care of his 12-year-old genius brother.

'Get Rich or Die Trying' (2005)

50 Cent started his acting career as early as 2005 when he starred in 'Get Rich or Die Trying'. The movie was a semi-autobiography of his own life. The movie script written by Terence Winter was produced by Jimmy Iovine, Paul Rosenberg, Chris Lighty and Jim Sheridan and was directed by Jim Sheridan. The movie's plot was based on the life of Marcus 'Young Caesar' Greer, the main

character who went into drug dealing after his mother dies in what looked like a drug deal gone wrong. Marcus' life takes many dark turns as he gets targeted by a drug kingpin, gets set up by his friend and eventually ends up in prison. While in prison, he makes a friend, Bama, who helps him discovers his passion and talent for rap. Bama encourages him to give up the life of crime, and Marcus decides to give his old ways up to fully pursue his true passion.

Since the makers of the movie had loosely based it on the life of Curtis Jackson, they enlisted his help in bringing the movie to life. 50 Cent played the role of Marcus 'Young Caesar' Greer, the main character. The movie also enlisted the help and talent of other great actors like Terrence Howard (who played Bama, the friend he made in prison), Joy Bryant (who played Charlene, his love interest), Bill Duke (who played Levar, the local drug Kingpin), Adewale Akinnuoye-Agbaje (who plays Majestic, Levar's underling), Omar Benson Miller (who plays Kyrl) and Viola Davis (who plays his grandmother).

The movie was released on November 9, 2005, made $12 million dollars in its opening weekend and a total of $46.4 million dollars at the box office. The movie did not get many favorable reviews from critics with many saying, that the rags to riches point of view had been overplayed and the producers of the movie were promoting an anti-intellectual message. Samuel L. Jackson very publicly denounced the movie after turning down a role in it saying that he did not believe that 50 Cent at the time was a good enough actor to be in the leading role.

'Home of the Brave' (2006)

50 Cent's next major movie role was in the 2006 drama, 'Home of the Brave'. The movie written, directed and produced by both Irvin Winkler and Mark Friedman, was based on the life of four soldiers and their lives after they returned to the United States from war-torn Iraq. The soldiers had experienced several explosions and battled insurgents for their lives. When they got back home, it

became increasingly difficult for them to adjust and assimilate into everyday life.

50 Cent joined other seasoned actors to bring this movie to life. The cast comprised of Samuel L. Jackson (who played Lieutenant Colonel Dr. William 'Will' Marsh M.D.), Jessica Biel (who played Sergeant Vanessa Price), Brian Presley (who played Specialist Tommy Yates), Chad Michael Murray (who played Private Jordan Owens), Christina Ricci (who played Sarah Schivino), Victoria Rowell (who played Penelope Marsh), Vyto Ruginis (who played Hank Yates) and Curtis '50 Cent' Jackson (who played Specialist Jamal Aiken).

This movie was not very well received at all, with movie review website currently giving a rating of only 22%. Only three movie theaters in the United States showed the movie, and it was only able to make $447,912 worldwide at the box office. The critics agreed that the cast tried very hard to give the movie some life, but the script they were handed just wasn't good enough.

Before I Self Destruct (2009)

In 2009, 50 Cent decided he wanted to write and produce his own movies. He wrote, directed, produced and executive produced his own movie, Self Destruct. Self Destruct, named after his fourth studio album, was about a young man, Clarence Jenkins (played by Curtis '50 Cent' Jackson) whose dreams of becoming a professional basketball player were cut short by a devastating knee injury. His mother (played by Donna Jenkins) dies shortly after in an accidental shooting, and he's left alone to support himself and his brother Shocka (played by Elijah 'Strong-E Williams) with his low-income supermarket job. He is eventually fired from this job and finds himself living a life of crime as a professional hitman. The movie explores the story of Clarence and what happens to him after he becomes rich from living a life of crime.

The cast included: Curtis '50 Cent' Jackson (who played Clarence Jenkins, the main character), Clifton Powell (who played

Sean, the local crime lord), Elijah 'Strong E' Williams (who played Shocka, Clarence's younger brother), Sasha Delvalle (who played Princess, Clarence's love interest), Gabriel Ellis (who played Rafael, Princess's dangerous ex-boyfriend), Shorty Red (who played Tiny, the man who killed Clarence's mother), Lloyd Banks (who played Shocka's school teacher), Kar (who played Donna Jenkins, Clarence's mother), Jaquan K.R. Cobb (who played Bobby, Shocka's best friend) amongst others.

The movie was written, produced and directed by Curtis '50 Cent' Jackson along with creative support from film producers like J. Jesses Smith, Ken Kushner and Frank Mosca.

All Things Fall Apart (2011)

Jackson didn't get any great role after *Get Rich* for a justifiable explanation: his performance was regarded as horrible.

Anxious to expand his acting range past his default job of "drug dealer in conventional spine chillers," Jackson made the strange and extraordinary act of shedding over 54 pounds and co-composing and specifically self-funding *All Things Fall Apart*, in which he plays a school football star who goes from being a genuine contender for the Heisman Trophy to getting a cancer diagnosis.

In 2011, 50 Cent starred in the movie, All Things Fall Apart. The movie written by Curtis Jackson and Brian A. Miller chronicles the life of Deon, a college football player who has to navigate college, family and football while dealing with a deadly disease, cancer. 50 Cent drew inspiration for this movie from the life of his childhood friend who passed away from cancer. 50 Cent put a lot of work and dedication into this movie, going as far as losing 54 pounds of weight in nine weeks. He reportedly achieved this by devoting himself to a strict liquid diet and running on a treadmill for 3 hours every single day. The end result was an emaciated looking Curtis

Jackson which successfully portrayed the cancer-ridden character, Deon.

That was an extraordinary commitment — particularly since 50 was a 35-year-old grown person playing the role of a school kid — however, regardless of whether he was brought into the world a similar day as his character, he, despite everything, wouldn't still have been able to bring the character to life. The frightening weight reduction course may work for prepared on-screen actors, yet the reaction to his search for reputability was equivalent to the reactions every one of his movies had: it was scarcely discharged in theaters and turned into a punchline for the pundits that Jackson had would have liked to dazzle. With *All Things Fall Apart,* Jackson attempted to build up himself as a thoughtful actor; rather he simply solidified his notoriety for being a hoodwinked egomaniac.

There was also some controversy over the title of the movie. 50 Cent initially wanted to title it 'Things Fall Apart' but that would have been infringing on the copyright of Nigerian author Chinua

Achebe and his 1958 novel with the same name. 50 Cent approached

Chinua Achebe's estate and offered them one million dollars for the

permission to keep 'Things Fall Apart' as the title of his movie. They

were however quite offended by the offer and rejected it. According

to them, the title of the most read book in modern African literature

was not up for sale, "not even for a billion dollars". Curtis Jackson

eventually resorted to changing the title of his movie from 'Things

Fall Apart' to 'ALL Things Fall Apart'.

The movie was produced by Randall Emmett, directed by

Mario Van Peebles and starred Curtis '50 Cent' Jackson (as Deon, the

main character), Ray Liotta (who played Dr. Brintall) and Mario Van

Peebles (as Eric, Deon's surrogate father). Other cast members

include Lynn Whitfield (who played Bee, Deon's mother), Ambyr

Childers (who played Sherry), Elizabeth Rodriguez (who played Mrs.

Lopez), Tracey Heggins (who played Sharon) and Steve Eastin.

The movie had a production budget of seven million dollars and was released on March 5, 2011, at the Miami International Film Festival.

Power (2014 – 2020)

Power is a crime drama that explores the character and story of James St. Patrick (played by Omari Hardwick). St. Patrick is a ruthless but brilliant drug lord masquerading as a legitimate night club owner and businessman in the day time. Known as *'Ghost'* in the criminal underworld, St. Patrick now wishes to leave the drug business and actually become a legitimate businessman.

The show follows St. Patrick as he navigates both worlds and tries to keep his family together in one piece while battling rivals like Kanan Stark (who is played by Curtis '50 Cent' Jackson). The show was created by Courtney A. Kemp and produced in collaboration with 50 Cent. It first aired on June 7, 2014, and 50 Cent even wrote the soundtrack for the series. 50 Cent was nominated for the NAMIC Vision Awards in the category of 'Best Performance – Drama' for his work in the series. The show and various actors in it have been nominated (and won) several awards over the course of its stay on television. 'Power' is one of 50 Cent's most successful attempts at Film and Television.

50 Cent has been involved in many more movies and television shows over the course of his career, even writing, directing and producing some.

At the point when *Power* initially debuted, nobody could tell how the TV series would do. A lot of persons knew 50 Cent as a rapper and were uncertain on the off-chance that he could pull off such a gigantic creating credit. Be that as it may, he advanced towards the job from an imaginative point of view.

"I'm not doing traditional on-set production," he said in 2015 at the Television Critics Association Press Tour. According to him, he keeps communication open with the talent, and he believes that when a producer participates in a series with the actors, a special is bond is created that enables open and free communication. In his words, when that bond is built, everyone feels comfortable to approach you and inform you of a problem before an additional problem is created.

50 Cent, THE ENTREPRENEUR

50 Cent is no stranger to success. Aside from the music 50 Cent explored and invested in other businesses leveraging his image and influence, making deals in a variety of industries from footwear to beverages. But he's now entering a new level of success via visual media. In fact, he's building an empire in the space, and it's buoyed by a cult of personality mixed with an uncanny ability to anticipate the interests of his target audience, that is, the very influential 80 million-plus Millennial demographic.

Very successful artistes are no longer with content with having their royalties as their solitary source of income. 50 Cent has taken being a multi-gifted tycoon with an enormous business domain to a whole new level.

He has utilized his prominence and his image to use his gifts as an unstoppable business visionary. 50 says, "once you're notable there is no opportunity to back off, you need to advertise the damnation out of yourself and get more presentation."

50 has made various a huge number of Dollars off the rear of his worldwide image. From books to nutrient water, 50 has cash rolling in from a ton of sources.

His approach as an entrepreneur is a definite game-changer that provides a great lesson for any entrepreneur making deals today.

Vitamin Water

One of 50's most worthwhile ventures was his arrangement with Vitamin Water. At the point when he signed an agreement to recommend the Formula 50 drink, the parent organization, Energy Bands, gave him a stake in the business. In the Spring of 2007, the organization was bought by Coca-Cola with 50's part of the arrangement being $100 Million even after expenses.

Headphones

Nine years ago, in 2011, 50 Cent established the earphones organization, SMS Audio, with SMS representing Studio Mastered Sound. In the late spring of that year, 50 bought KonoAudio, at a price that still remains confidential.

The Headphone business keeps on being a development region for 50, with his organization being the lead in remote earphones and later associations with Basketball Star Carmelo Anthony propose further development.

Books

50 Cent's secretly composed collection of memoirs *From Pieces to Weight* purportedly sold up to 100,000 duplicates with complete transactions of $1.9 Million.

His most recent book, *The 50TH Law* sees him working together with *The 48 Laws of Power* writer, Robert Greene.

"I didn't go to Harvard but the people that work for me did" – 50 Cent.

Energy Shots

50 Cent has joined forces with Pure Growth Partners to make the enhanced caffeinated drink Street King, presently known as SK Energy. The caffeinated drink has had a few prominent benefactors including Floyd Mayweather, Mike Tyson and Joan Rivers, prompting an expanded profile for the organization.

50 Cent likewise utilizes the benefits from each shot bought to contribute meals through the World Food Program.

Clothing

In the year 2003, 50 Cent collaborated with Mark Ecko Enterprises to make garments that was sold through Ecko Limited. Before going separate ways in 2008, G-Unit Clothing was answerable for 15% of Ecko's income. With the garments and caps acquiring $75

Million in   2006, 50 Cent's 8% equity implied that he made $6

Million that year alone.

The Rest of 50 Cent's Empire

Music, books, nutrient water, earphones, caffeinated beverages and apparel is not sufficient enough for 50 Cent. In all honesty, there is a lot more to his empire than those. 50 Cent has acted with Al Pacino, Robert De Niro and Forest Whittaker in his rising vocation as an entertainer and has even begun his own film production organization.

50 has additionally sold $125 Million+ worth of computer games after the title, Bulletproof sold in an abundance of 2.5 Million Copies. Just as with garments, 50 was paid over $20 Million by Reebok in 2003 to not just invest his planning prowess, but also his image in another line of tennis shoes. The tennis shoes wound up being a massive hit, producing more than $320 Million. 50 Cent has made no mystery of his craving to be a Billionaire and helpful for this, he likewise keeps on building his Real Estate and Financial Portfolios.

Becoming a highly successful entrepreneur, among other things, does not happen by chance. There is a lot of underground work that the public does not usually get to see.

How did 50 Cent do it?

50 Cent is Connected.

To be sure, this man has a reputation. He appears to realize what will be hot and placed all his business energies around there, and it pays off. Perhaps the biggest arrangement was the money out from Glaceau after Coca-Cola coincidentally purchased the organization for $4.1 billion. Jackson, who was a minority investor in the organization, earned $100 million from the arrangement after duties, as per Forbes, on water.

DJ Kast One, on-air personality at New York's leading hip hop radio Hot 97's, knows Jackson and has had him on his show many times. "Basically, 50 is successful because he has the ability to know what people want, even a type of water. He can see what direction things are going, in terms of trends and interests, and can move toward it. This was evident in his clothing line."

Be that as it may, Kast One says that what truly invigorates 50 Cent is that he can keep up a similar degree of honesty, or "realness" regardless of all his prosperity. It's this ability that gives him his edge.

50 Cent is a Visionary & Authentic

Randall Emmett, who produced movies like Rambo, Heist, and Amityville Horror and is also 50 Cent's production partner affirms this point and believes he is a visionary based on the moves 50 Cent has made over the years with brands he partnered with or created himself like the Effen Vodka and the deal with Vitamin Water.

The two men met up in light of the fact that quite a long while back, 50 understood that Hollywood was not composing any jobs for him, so he basically chose to make his own. Presently Emmett and Curtis produce various shows and movies independently and together, one of which is the tremendously well-known crime drama, *Power*.

50 Cent is Supportive

Emmet also commented on 50 Cent's knack for supporting teammates to be successful and also brands he works with. According to Emmet, when networks work with 50 Cent, he is 100% committed to the project as a partner.

According to Emmett, that's the only way he believes 50 Cent knows how to work.

Emmett has a lot of stories about 50 Cent going the extra mile to try and loan his own picture and accessibility for photo shoots and more for advertising and advancement for Emmett's work even when it was not associated with 50 Cent.

50 Cent is Direct

The real deal about 50 Cent is that he is fearless. "Let's face it. 50 has no problem lighting people up," laughs Emmett.

Without a doubt, when things got somewhat rough with negotiations for the renewal of his crime drama series, *Power*, 50 Cent chose to accomplish something that very few TV power players could ever do. He made his fans a part of the arrangements through his Instagram feed by mentioning to them what was actually happening and proposing that they really drop their membership to the cable network. The deals then worked in his favor, and he gave his fans the go-ahead to re-subscribe to the cable network and afterward boasted about it with fellow celeb Denzel Washington.

50 Cent Embraces Change

At the point when piracy of music was at an all-time high, the music industry made a lot of effort suing many music platforms, for example, Napster and Kaza, to court, doing whatever they could to keep music from being distributed at no cost.

But 50 Cent? He did not even move a muscle. He didn't whine or even grumble about people for pilfering his music. He considered it to be a chance to develop. He took to the Mixtape circuit and began informally remixing others' records, with a piece of his own creativity, to flavor it up. Individuals got on to the remixes and went gaga for 50 and his G-Unit group practically overnight.

50 Cent Is Highly Resourceful

After 50 Cent broke into the music business, he utilized his income towards investing and buying shares in growing businesses. He began his own attire line and collaborated with Reebok and made the G-Unit tennis shoes.

Ecko now owns the line, and it is still unfathomably effective today. He spread out and began organizing with business tycoons and extremely rich people, discovering the best and most worthwhile businesses to invest in.

50 Cent Loves Taking Risks

50 Cent is presumably the most well-known for his association with Glaceau's Vitamin Water brand. In return for recommending the product, he was granted a minority stake in the organization and wound up winning over $100 million from Coca-Cola's $4.1 billion acquisition of the brand.

He didn't need to invest his cash, however, he needed to invest both his image and reputation.

50 Cent is Willing To Give Back

Not too long ago, 50 Cent changed it up and took the charity route. Utilizing the assets from his caffeinated drink brand, SK Energy Shots, he is presently utilizing his items as an approach to give back by cooperating with Feeding America and SMS Audio. For each pair of SYNC by 50 and STREET by 50 earphones sold online, SMSAudio.com will give 250 meals that will take care of families in America.

50 Cent Never Sets Limits On What He Can Achieve

Another reason for 50 Cent's highly successful entrepreneurial journey is that he doesn't restrict himself. Just recently, he became a licensed boxer promoter and also got a deal with Right Guard to produce body deodorant. He also produced a caffeinated drink brand, as well as an earphone brand. Curtis also got involved in the production of a condom line called Magic Stick Condoms and also possesses a film organization where he acted with a couple of Hollywood action stars and royalties like Bruce Willis, Jason Statham, Chase Crawford and a few others.

50 Cent Is Self-Reliant

50 Cent lost his mom at an exceptionally young age, and he also never knew his dad. This constrained 50 Cent to need to turn out to be increasingly autonomous on the off-chance that he needed to make it in this world.

Instead of waiting to be dependent on the entertainment and business industries, 50 Cent made his own chances and turned into his own boss. Rather than rely on others, he became reliant on himself.

50 Cent Stays Engaged With His Fans & Followers

50 Cent keeps on engaging his fan base all the time. By keeping his customers up to date on his business projects and investments, he is guaranteeing his own success. He keeps in touch with his followers and also keeps them up to date through his Instagram and Twitter accounts every now and then. He understands that his followers are more than just his music industry groupies. His potential for progress is solid as long as he stays associated with the outside world of his fans, knowing and understanding their needs, so he can situate himself in the most ideal organizations where there are worthwhile ventures and levels of popularity.

50 Cent Surrounds Himself With Successful Individuals

There is no uncertainty that 50 Cent has made a great deal of accomplishment, yet he likewise recognizes that he was unable to have done it without anyone else. He has assembled an exceptionally solid group around him comprising of fruitful and learned individuals. He assigns undertakings to people around him with the goal that he can, in any case, proceed to construct himself as an entertainer, yet in addition, have the option to search out the next successful business project.

50 Cent Stands Proudly Behind His Products

50 Cent won't promote, recommend, or remain behind an item except if he genuinely has faith in it. This has been the main

consideration of his entrepreneurial success. On the off-chance that you don't have confidence in the item at that point, there is no trouble in supporting it. 50 Cent accepts, that in the event that he can't remain behind something, general society can tell, which will mean fluctuating achievement.

50 Cent Follows His Passions

Furthermore, 50 Cent chases his dreams with an unbelievable measure of energy, making him a relentless power to be dealt with. He has faith in himself and has resolute confidence in his work. He is knowledgeable and ready to become familiar with the business he is in and never gets excessively okay with what he has.

He just takes on ventures that he can identify with and can completely put stock in.

During an ABC interview, when he was asked how young black people could get ahead of obstacles and terminate the feeling of hopelessness, he advised you should have something you are passionate about and do it.

Discovering his interests and chasing his dreams permits him to arrive at the most significant level of progress.

50 Cent's Multimillion-Dollar Deal

A year ago, the rapper made millions of dollars by signing a four-year in general arrangement with Starz. In the understanding, it expresses that 50 Cent will keep on making scripted and unscripted shows for the cable network through the G-Unit Film and TV.

This deal included a three-series commitment, along with the use of discretionary funds for developing his projects.

According to Variety, this deal could have been worth as much as $150 million.

How much does 50 Cent make for "?

No exact details have been released on how much 50 Cent makes from *Power*, but according to Glassdoor, TV executive producers make an average of $146,538. But judging from the fact that 50 Cent also stars in the show, that amount is probably significantly higher.

Things you probably did not know about *Power*.

Regardless of the fact that the series only officially got to the UK as a Netflix-licensed show in 2016, 50 Cent's abrasive crime drama dramatization rapidly became one of the most well-known shows on television.

50 Cent does not simply show up as an entertainer in *Power*; he is likewise the executive producer of the show. The rapper is supposedly very involved in the show's production. He utilized his own individual encounters from his own life to support the show and his own character Kanan.

The *Power* cast visited 50 Cent's old New York neighborhood for motivation. Omari Hardwick, who played Ghost, and Joseph Sikora, who played Tommy, both hung out in 50 Cent's old neighborhood Jamaica, in Queens, for a couple of nights to ensure that their portrayal of their jobs were depictions were true. "Joe and I did Jamaica, Sovereigns, two evenings in succession. Late, late, 3 a.m. in the first part of the day late," Hardwick said.

Naturi Naughton, who plays Phantom's better half, Tasha, in the show, was really one of the first members from R&B trio 3LW. She showed up on the group's platinum-selling self-titled presentation collection.

The New York area is essential to the show. 50 Cent experienced his childhood in Jamaica, Queens and needed *Power* to have a lumpy, credible vibe that is one of a kind to New York. "It's bricks, it's day off's, solid, it's hot around evening time, odd-looking during the day. It's dismal. It's Gotham City!" Omari Hardwick, who plays Ghost, said. "Our objective was to make this show with that name appended to it be not mushy and be simply truly something that lone any semblance of The Sopranos are."

The fourth season of *Power* was shockingly stopped. Season four of *Power* was sliced short because of a contest between 50 Cent and Television station Starz. The season's emotional end was constrained into two scenes, as Starz would not permit the show to air any additional scenes.

50 Cent's private region was exposed during the third season of the show. 50 Cent was allegedly vexed after his manhood was left exposed by mistake during the third season of the show. In any case,

he got over it during an interview meeting with TVGuide.com. "I don't give a f**k", he said. "First it should be darker [after the film was edited.] You couldn't see it on the screen." [A producer] said, 'I gotta show you! At the point when you put it on the screen, you can see it.' I don't care'.

Power has a gigantic fight with Fox Television program, *Empire*. Notwithstanding the fact that these are two different shows on completely different networks, Power and Starz are furious opponents. In the previous years, 50 Cent has exchanged not so serious shade, through social media with Taraji P. Henson, who plays Cookie in *Empire.*

The show is nearly as well-known as HBO's *Game Of Thrones.* In May 2017, Deadline uncovered that *Power* was the most famous show on premium cable after HBO's *Game of Thrones.* Such accomplishment!

Proctor additionally showed up as Turtle in HBO's *Entourage*. Jerry Ferrara, who plays Ghost's lawyer, Joe Proctor, is additionally most popular for his featuring job as Turtle in HBO's award-winning show *Entourage*.

There is a tremendous measure of the Spanish language in the show to reflect New York City. *Power* needed to speak for the huge Latino people group in New York reasonably and in this manner chose to include loads of Spanish-talking individuals. The creator of the show, Courtney Kemp Agboh stated: "To have Dominican, Cuban, Mexican entertainers be from where they are from... that was my obsession, and Starz was absolutely behind me on that despite the fact that it's detail work that individuals don't generally do."

The last episode of the fourth season of *Power* arrived at a record-breaking viewership.

In spite of 50 Cent confessing to spilling episodes before they were released, the fourth season of the show finished on a record high. The last episode of the show got a group of people reaching almost 1.9 million, making it a season-high and the fifth most elevated number in its history.

Things Most People Might Not Know About Curtis "50 Cent" Jackson

He doesn't drink, do drugs or smoke.

This is probably one of the most shocking facts about the controversial rapper whose song and videos depict the elements of drugs and drinks. 50 Cent even owns a champagne company, but the rapper in an interview with Piers Morgan, said although he sold drugs at a young age, but abstained from it.

Also, he mentioned that he had an experience with alcohol that made him wary of the substance, making him stay away from it despite often rapping about it.

For instance, he was asked about the authenticity of one of the tracks *'High all the time'* on the *'Get rich or die trying'* album despite his claim of not doing drugs or taking alcohol. He replied that the reason he put the elements of drug and alcohol in the song was that it was what was popular at that moment, and they obviously helped to sell more records.

"I put that joint on the first record because I saw artists consistently selling 500,000 with that content."[1]

His first dog was killed by his Aunt.

50 Cent loved dogs, but at a young age, 50 Cent has a rather ugly experience with his canine after his Aunty killed his dog by putting roach spray in a bowl used by the dog thereby killing the dog and 50 Cent said it was because his Aunty didn't like him growing up.

In the club **bought him Mike Tyson's house.**

'*In the club*' single was one of the most successful singles from the '*Get rich or die trying*' album and got 50 Cent a lot of accolades and returns.

It was part of the proceeds which he used in purchasing Mike Tyson 50,000 square feet mansion.

He has some of the most expensive cars in the world

[1] http://rollingout.com/music/50 Cent-cent-lied-about-smoking-weed-to-sell-records/2/

50 Cent is a big fan of cars, and from his fleet of cars are some of the most expensive auto-machines in the world. 50 Cent has as part of his fleet, some Ferraris, G8, Rolls Royce, and Lamborghini Murcielago.

50 Cent favorite verse ever is not from one of his own songs

Normally, if you were at an interview where 50 Cent was asked what is a favorite verse of all time was, without a doubt, you would expect to hear something from *'Get rich or die trying'*, *'Massacre'* or *'Curtis'*, but on the contrary, 50 Cent's favorite verse ever is not from any one of his songs. His favorite verse, which he revealed on a show "This is 50", was a single *'The Message'* from Nas's 1996 album *'It was written'*.

50 Cent produced a series title *For life* for ABC after STARZ refused it

Although *Power* is probably the most successful 50 Cent has ever produced but what most people might not know was that he also produced another successful series titled *For life'* which was based on the true-life story of Isaac Wright Jr. who was sentenced to 70 years in jail for a crime he didn't commit. While speaking during an interview on ABC about when he pitched the series to executives at STARZ, who are the producers of *Power*, they refused it and ABC bought it, and according to him, they were shocked as to how successful the series became.

He has a star on the Hollywood Walk of Fame.

Earlier this year, Curtis "50 Cent" Jackson was honored with a star on the Hollywood walk of fame. An honor that is usually bestowed on individuals in the entertainment industry who have achieved considerable milestones in the industry.

Origin of the name "50 Cent"

By 1996, after Curtis was signed by RUN D.M.C, he adopted the name 50 Cent, a name which was inspired by a petty criminal by the name of Kelvin Martin, who used the same name. When asked why he chose the name, he said he chose it because it was a metaphor for change, which implied that he was going to do things his own way that was drastically different from the way others did. In his words, "the name says everything he wanted to say because he had the same 'go-getter' attitude as the original 50 Cent."

How to Rob

This record was off his unreleased album '*Power of the dollar*' which was recorded in 1998 and was set for release in 2000 but was never released by Columbia Records, which was 50 Cent's label at the time because of the nine bullets incident which led to the label terminating his contract.

The single was released in 1999 and was one of the most sensational tracks off the album and one of the records that shot him to the limelight. The song talked about how he was going to rob hip hop stars and really caused a stir in the industry. Eminem said when he heard the record, he knew he (50 Cent) was going to make a lot of enemies. The record drew a lot of attention even Jay Z had to fire back a reply.

The 9 Bullet story

Most people know that 50 Cent was shot nine times, but there are parts that most people don't know about the incident. For instance, during the shooting, 50 Cent said he had a gun while he was being shot at, and while he tried to fire back, he discovered that the gun was not cocked. Also, another thing most people might know is that the doctors who were operating on 50 Cent tried to carry out a tracheotomy, a procedure which involved them opening 50 Cent's wide pipe and which could potentially destroy his chances of ever rapping again.

His grandma, however, refused. She said, "If he couldn't do his music, he would be lost."

Some two weeks after the incident, a man named Darryl Baum, who also happened to be a former bodyguard to Mike Tyson, was found dead although no connection to 50 Cent's shooting was made.

Puff Daddy

It might sound as a surprise to most, but the first person that offered to sign 50 Cent after his label, Columbia records dumped him was Sean "Diddy" Combs who offered him a job as a songwriter, but according to 50 Cent on the day he went to visit Diddy, there was an altercation happening outside Diddy's office, and Diddy stepped in, 50 Cent pulled his gun.

His reason? He was paranoid, and according to him, he wasn't ready to be shot a second time.

Kanye West

50 Cent was not an entertainer and an avid businessman, but he was also someone who knew how to do PR and capitalize on controversies.

One of the incidents where he exhibited the knack for turning controversies to his advantage was when in 2007, while promoting his third album 'Curtis', he made an unprecedented move.

He announced publicly that if Kanye West sold more albums than his album (both albums were due to be released on the same date), he was going to quit music, and the fans bought into the challenge, thereby helping the both of them make good sales off their album.

When 50 Cent was asked in an interview about the results of the challenge and how he felt about Kanye emerging the winner, 'Kanye west gets the trophy, 50 gets the checks'.

He has never really killed anyone.

There is no evidence on record that 50 Cent killed anyone although some try to tie the death of Daryll Baum to him, because he was the hitman who almost cost him his life by shooting him nine times but there is no evidence to prove it.

And his shooting history is almost non-existent as the only time it was reported that he shot someone was when some kids tried to rob in school, and he shot one of them.

50 Cent has never really been in prison.

Despite his gangster outlook, 50 Cent has never really been to prison. Although there was a period where he was arrested for possession of drugs (which he sold) in his home and was sentenced about nine years in jail, but he was sent to a boot camp for six months where he earned his GED and got out.

Since then, he hasn't been convicted.

Conclusion

Curtis "50 Cent" Jackson is an interesting personality, and there is no doubt that his life story is one that would inspire many, especially those from rough, humble backgrounds. Some of his moves and challenges just point to the fact that impossible is nothing, and it's more than just the common aspirational and grass to grace stories we hear. 50's story is an authentic one which most hustlers can relate to.

Final Surprise Bonus

Final words from the author...

Hope you've enjoyed this biography of 50 Cent.

It was an utmost privilege performing deep research and bringing forth these information to the public for you to enjoy.

I always like to overdeliver, so I'd like to give you one final bonus.

Do me a favor, if you enjoyed this book, please leave a review on Amazon.

It'll help get the word out so more people can find out more about our beloved superstar to support his legacy! (Plus, it'll help me a lot too. Thanks in advance!)

If you do, as a way of way of saying "thank you", I'll send you one of my most cherished collection report– Free:

50 Cent: The Complete Discography Collection From The Beginning to the Very End

A complete list of all of 50 Cent's work that was ever published (or not published). As a 50 Cent fan, you'll find this utmost valuable and cannot be missed!

Here's how to claim your free report:

1. Leave a review right away on Amazon (longer the better but I'd be grateful for whatever length).

2. Send a screenshot to: jjvancebooks@gmail.com

3. Receive your free report –"**The Complete Discography Collection From The Beginning to the Very End**"–*immediately*!

Enjoyed This Book? Then Check Out...

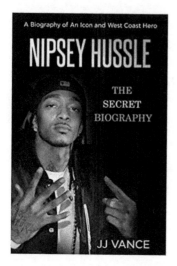

Get to know the "Real" Nipsey Hussle - Behind the Music

Here's Just a Taste What You're About to Read in This Concise Nispey Hussle Biography:

Nipsey Hussle's Personal Life

Hussle has a daughter named Emani from a previous relationship. He dated actress Lauren London from 2013 till his death in 2019. They have a son named Kross together, who was born on the 31st of August, 2016.

What paved the way for their long-term love story was when London wanted to buy Hussle's mixtapes for her co-stars. After getting the tapes, she began following him on Instagram and he also followed her in return. They began their relationship after some time.

Nipsey recently praised Lauren for the sacrifice she made for their family. John Singleton picked her for Snowfall. She got the role, shot the pilot and even performed stunts. This was a dream role for her. However, she had to make an extremely tough decision when she started expecting their son. She chose their family.

Lauren also has a 9-year-old son Cameron with Lil Wayne. Nipsey and Lauren tried their best to keep their children away from the spotlight. They usually did not post their children's pictures on social media, with only a few exceptions. When they appeared in GQ in white clothes on a horse, it sparked engagement rumors.

A great tribute to a true hero that transcended music!

Check it out here:

https://jjvance.com/NipseyHussle

Or Scan the QR Code: